Roller Coasters Made of Dream Space

100 poems

by

Peter J. Dellolio

"Make visible what, without you, might perhaps never have been seen."
--Robert Bresson

ISBN: 978-81-19654-40-6

First Edition: 2023
Rs. 200/-

Cyberwit.net
HIG 45 Kaushambi Kunj, Kalindipuram
Allahabad - 211011 (U.P.) India
http://www.cyberwit.net
Tel: +(91) 9415091004
E-mail: info@cyberwit.net

Printed at Repro India Limited.

For My Grandparents,

Amelia and Rocco Constantino

Frances and Orazio Dellolio

Contents

Muscularity Diary

muscularity
diary shouting insults
into Larry's tool chest
    but you should take it easy
    Larry
    there was sufficient
    clarity in the clarinet
        box

    quintet jackass fuse
    a short temper
    flaws in the animal's jaws

mendacity
quarry mounting rivets
give us the sunset
ride the lorry

    sometimes toothpick
    stem fumbling creates
    God music in a
    red experiment room
use antique railroad lanterns
to search for Larry because
he's as thin as an air shaft

            breeze

Cuckoo Clock Conveyor Belt

cuckoo clock
conveyor belt
so
eyelid meal in
the sponge spaceship
all the time
and with
brine
there is
banter?

stop complaining
about the beast coins
knockabout
alfalfa syrup made
her more buxom in
the stirrups and I
cannot
endorse *Salami Joe*
in the new
election

they murdered a
refrigerator that was wearing a tan fish mask
not the best of days
in the land of rubber magic
the tragic
dimensions of the transom
and the talcum harem
had a banquet tantrum
in the land of phantoms

They Were Busy Tossing

they
were busy tossing
a *Colorforms* salad
next to the eerie
fortune teller
lady in her box
under the
Wonder Wheel

and a key lime pie whistle
brisket was marauding
through
the
thicket although munching
syringe binges
were quieted by
minor harmonies
followed by saliva
blocks cheating the
wood in the kindergarten
play chest

so they could not rest
because
they
were dizzy crossing
a valor-torn mallard

special night fix, huh?
onward, voyager!
wayward dowager

You Forgot

you forgot
to
leave yourself
some
wiggle room
and
the question
is
who was
doing
the talking
I
mean who
was
speaking to
whom
not too
far
to look
because
there were
only
three parties
involved:

the dirt
the broom

and

the wall

The Spider Webs

the spider webs
flexed and rippled
like rows of little
white waves
it was the haunted
Superman lunch box
and a miasmic puppet
went on a hunger
strike for the express
purpose of stripping hat fat
off of the granite
totem pole
    are you insane?
    there weren't any vacuum
    nodules on the underside
    of
    The Monster That
    Challenged the World
    I suppose *Tim Holt*
    had an excuse to get
    chubby
that is, there weren't any cowboys
        around, either
        to poke fun at him,
                you know?

We Slowly and Quietly Floated

we slowly and quietly floated
past a cluster of pale blue
wooden tables and
orange test tubes
and
powdery pink sledge hammers and
fire-engine red hammocks
and then *Spencer Tracy*
used karate to beat up
Ernest Borgnine in that
great scene from
Bad Day at Black Rock
and
we drifted towards
maroon diving boards
and turquoise
chef hats and
green black
boards and yellow
limousines
with bakelite
steering wheels
limestone hub caps
walnut windshields
and
magnesium mufflers

The Shades on the Windows

the shades on the
windows
were those black and gray
test screens from
the 50s and 60s
with the profile of
the American Indian
everyone at the party had
clubfoot
no, I mean
accordions for feet
stale chop meat ankles
musical flesh
oboe ventricle
obligations of nautical sour
what a dream
facsimile of
pewter rental an
infection not to be
confused
with
confessions of a
twisted pumpkin taken to
the scary old house
tortured
until
Tonsil Tommy said
"Tinsel Tessie Tessler
gives it away on Christmas
Eve!"

Guillotine Pimples

guillotine pimples
tried, but you gotta
get there by yourself,
Mack, nobody can
fix the rackets like
they used to in *Stromboli*
and if they throw red
white and blue stones at
Ingrid while she's
Viaggio in Italia
then all those *morte*
yachts can go to rust
in dreamy and dust some
mean tea while you're at it

Thunder Bike Mike

thunder bike Mike was washing a tall
radioactive chocolate malted
over in the
Howdy Doody
plastic overalls factory
when
Joe
and
Bea told
a juniper gent to gently quit stealing
from Kent
and I mean Clark, goddammit!
not *King Lear's* drop of earl!
that's all, Punch!
and screw you, too, Judy!

There is a Morbid Organ Grinder

there is a morbid
organ grinder deep
in one of the
pyramids from
Land of The Pharaohs

hurry to ask him
questions about how
Toland lit *Citizen*
Kane because in
about ten seconds
Bettie Page's S&M
costume is going to
fly down the paper
mache steps leading
into the burial chamber
and forever distract
the grinder man from
faithfully performing
his duties

and what are these
sacred ministrations?

penultimate nap soda
fire on the mantle
diapers with ozone
nectar vapor locked

box *Zoot* suit in
the *Cabrini* rose destiny

hope those bandages aren't
too
tight
Tut

They Electrocuted a Rogue Elephant

they
electrocuted
a rogue elephant
it's on film
in black and white
early twentieth century
he went bad
they said
Coney Island rampaging
elephant
killed some men

watching the film is like
a little boy yanked out of his
bed
put into a sack in the middle
of the night
you can see parts of the tents
there were clowns walking
around as the elephant suddenly
shuddered and fell over like a giant wave
having a heart attack
they put the boy back into
the room
but he was beaten
his bed turned into a furnace
and the faces on
all his
toys
were
gone

Special Wagon Minister

special
wagon minister
rope full of soap
for a dope like you
or a wretch like me
there is ocular
constipation under the gravy flags
of *Jerry Mahoney* nations
in the *Silly Putty*
codebook
and
should you look into
dirty nooks and crannies
you will find *Bette Davis*
in *The Nanny*
it's bath time
for ruptured entrée missiles
covered in thistle
and coal

There is Madness in the Iodine

there is madness in the iodine
buttercup mystery
an enigma of grayish-white
entrails or slice brains
without the blood
blanched cross section
the sky full of fat unfolding clouds
after the rain
looking like body parts on *Gray's* dissection table

An Argument Against Lasciviousness

an argument against lasciviousness
with the freckles on the face
of the little boy brought before
the expressionistically large
desk at the police station *Invaders*
From Mars is the movie and
who we
mesmerize with our
splendor eyes
is quite another matter
did you seriously mean
"splendorize"?
I think that's bad English and
in any event
special Navy blankets give nightmares

to rubber grasshopper symphonies
did they actually mean
"sympathy for phonies"?
I think "actually"
used in this way
is a split infinitive
but I'm not sure

do we really want to put
"splints into the infinite"?

Nice Brown Butcher Paper

nice
brown
        butcher paper
        and thick string tightly wound
        around and around
        a Merry-Go-Round of
                stains
                of meat blood

Severity of the Chicken

severity
of the chicken in noxious
luscious litanies
forever mangled in the mumbling
dungeon
so you see
it
was an inarticulate road
map that slapped *Don Juan's*
boiling white
piano
not a tendril sandwich because I am
the rendezvous mischief mustard
not Venetian custard
and I take umbrage
at such a suggestion
that's just fine!
so we'll take your umbrella, fella!
kudos to *Mephistopheles* for embryonic
embroidery doilies
mistakenly dolled up by
oily birds getting the
germ

There is a Glass of White Wine

there
is a glass of white wine
glistening
a burning orange-yellow
sunset dinner at the
end of the dock
those crisscrossing
white sailboats are
opposite ends of a
jovial harmonium
and deck hands with compact
black caps are
the notes
buttons of melody being pressed to
make music for
fried scallops to be dipped in
liberally seasoned
Beijing sauce
soberly tossed mushroom caps
commingling with Russian
dance hats and triple
servings of triumvirate
nozzle passages cooked with
Luden's
sausages
with bandages following the
Adagio for Strings
by *Samuel Barber* so if you need a haircut
listen to *Albinoni* instead

So What?

so what?
maybe Plato liked burgers
from those roadside diners
giving lectures on his back
probably before
The Rifleman got cancelled
just another way
to
make
ends meat

Broken Coffee Horror

broken
coffee
horror all ship
tonsils in the wooden
slop market
you! target
splash! to get
another eyeball to weep for Angela
her fragrant small helmets in soft
pajamas
I, *Mama Tombs*
to nuzzle in drizzle
with wet whips Wendy!
and
Haydn handling it
more than ninety times
my my

Spruced Up Wrinkle Farts

spruced up
wrinkle farts
mixed with
watered down
syndrome in
the astrodome
you can call it
home
on
the
range or split peas
with *Pee-wee*
but orange motor cars
gesticulating in front of
maiden
list jars of
young girl lapidary
diaries
or dire
nunneries
it must rewind before
Frosty melts
and bad boys use his
empty derby
for a
Druid sacrifice

Caution Cauldrons

caution
cauldrons were not bison
underway, anyway?

a bridge under
construction
functioning *Mumbles*
straitjacketed *Tracy*
anyway, strait away?

hypodermic
pachyderm
roaming around nonsense
Sen-Sen
soapy repeated, bleated?

lamb lamps on fire
in the middle
of a choir
dream knots
fathoms
in league with
the Devil
with you, Woodrow?

Wilson!
Wilson!
Wilson!

Crisp Quintet Darkness

crisp
quintet darkness
in the hallway noose
of soup, do you think?
I will be at the
funeral. They installed
a miniature
movie screen inside
the coffin. There is
a double feature tonight:
Bride of the Gorilla
and
The
Graduate
so ineptitude won't cause
gratitude in the slaughtered
brood
regardless of any
hallucinating forest
jam session
a cessation
of kleptomaniacal
cackling
in the
blue marble
museum of
transformed
dummy
horns

Somersaults and Meatballs

somersaults
and
meatballs
win the *Chopin*
sewing machine
it's over there, far away in the clandestine
hiatus puncture
will get us
nowhere, Monsieur
no, I meant
that I
miss your
smile,
your dance,
yore tropism is the schism that Jim
was beaming about
I mean
before the trout cabin
murders began
you know
the ones which
Stan begat
before
the
bracket
brigade
took
over and,
in Dover,
there is clover.

It's Like That *Outer Limits* Episode

it's like that
Outer Limits
episode
where *Eddie Albert*
tries to talk
to the tumble weeds
nobody can hear your sobs
maybe music
in the luncheonette
a big green bakelite
blender to
make a nice ice cold chocolate shake
in one of those thick
V-shaped
glasses
and I'll you tell you something...
it got really weird when
Eddie put the frog in the basin
of water
and it dissolved
poof!
just like that
so if a truck driver
wearing a steamy germ
turban
offered you a free ride to
Portsmouth,

would you accept?
    I bet you would and
            in
            sotto voce
            to boot!

Oranges So Much

oranges
so much
and the navy blue place
        I think
        almost all of the
        trunks
        were
tiger maple
I don't think she likes
oranges so much anymore
now that
mischief beyond the grave
        navy
        blue cashmere scarf
        in that place
        no no no
don't place so much importance
on the oranges because I think
that mischief in that place
cannot be ruled out it's a
promiscuous boarding school (my
God! *Joan Crawford's* daughter,
Cristina, went there!) and they
will only get insanely jealous
of such expensive luggage (dear
Lord! who ever heard of tiger
maple, custom made trunks!) so I
would pack the cashmere scarf

the fall is awfully chilly over there
it's a grave decision but I
think the Navy academy is a much
better choice even if she is blue for a time

We'd Like to Assail

we'd like to assail the shiny
copper
pail of snails
and the smell
of wood is like
a photograph
of lunar succulence
a dense dance of crab caps
or
lobster voodoo figures
taking deep sea diving
lessons
play in the string quartet
OK?
let's let *Rigoletto* into
the *Hindu*
Trigger Museum so *Roy*
and *Dale*
can see him
all decked out
loud lawn necklace
strangles
melted coal dartboard
details
at
11

Last One in the Shower

last one in the shower
is a somnambulistic
prop manager
on the set of an *Abbott & Costello*
gorilla movie
and his left foot is
cynical from years of wrist watch
brain cell juggling while
splendid movie popcorn fought
with *Benny Goodman*
because his clarinet
was really black opium with
silver candy holes
now
I suppose the producer of the
gorilla movie liked having a secret
rendezvous with the
prop manager but
I was always enchanted by that
Slinky
commercial
it was the way the long spring
flopped down and over
from step to step

False Lemon Leaning

false lemon leaning
against Leonard
just so you know
with paste or shimmer
his dinner is *Phase IV*
behemoth nonsense
all sands wren speck!

GI Sandwich Town

GI sandwich town the
yodel expensive gift
to the masticating
missive no *Elmer Fudd* is
whipping Indonesian
puppets so tough it
out on the range
where my dear pantalone
                    play

Skinflint Beard Hunt

skinflint beard hunt and
no it's not Mike Hunt
bust of savor in the manger
for dolphin messages all
nocturnal journals hide it's
true *Beave*, *Wally* likes to
mumble in front of old
machinery

Too Bad

too bad his jacket band
got caught on the door
that's what happens when
you play chicken a dream
of the hot rods thundering
into the night probably those
few seconds of life left
in Jimmy's severed head
after *The Spyder* did him in

Smoke Tuck of the Turk

smoke tuck of the Turk
in such a jaunty jasmine box
loitering of soiled souls
leapt all tidy taxing the
patience of *The All Mighty*
it's porcelain paintings
puncturing piccolo tonsils
and someone smoked all
the eyelids

Incantation

incantation of can't
soldering nephew banister
all rolled up so nicely
I'm a rug roller from
Raleigh, damn you! Sift
through the hamlet for an
omelet of *Manifest Destiny*
regurgitation of *Kant*

Leapt for the Screw

leapt for the screw my
snarl Lin such anger
for a dainty Chinese
beauty give smacks to
the mackerel so the
mischief muscles will donate
blood to the tussled
hair factory

Rescued Teepee Hospital

rescued teepee hospital
salt with so much
fake fuss for you
I am robust at twilight
and the tarantula
circus is leaving
swollen shadows on
the rubber gray moon

Harmony Leather

harmony leather of the
sweat stain on
soiled brown boxing gloves
plenty of pigeon lectures on
the orange clay tennis
courts without musky
malice because Alice
rubbed the chalice with
her charms

He Said Madness Lies There

he said madness lies there
like going into the wrong
room only the door shuts
behind you kind of like the
post office scene from
1408 and *Cusack*
thinks he's out of the nightmare
what a shock when the
room emerges like screaming
disfigurement after cosmetic
surgery gone terribly wrong

Butter Blocks

butter blocks accusing
mustache bubbles of
sexual *Neptune* nectar
and old ladder daze
next to the chewing
tobacco flesh fence
not a second more
mind you, the bulls eye
serenade lemonade is
in the shade

We Cannot Rent the Ventricle Bazooka

we cannot rent the
ventricle bazooka next
month so *Malignant Mario*
and the *Turpentine Toy Box*
will have to mobilize another
clam prize and somnambulant
eyes will dazzle no more

She Wore

she wore a very short
very sexy Italian spruce
skirt and there was
vulture blood on the
gorgeous soft sensuous
white bear skin rug
so I sniffed the
toasted sort of peppery
smell of the *Lucky*
Strike cigarette before
I smoked it and
her wooden skirt
woke up the people
across the hall because
leaflets insult
bed poles every
time the ringmaster
smiles

Bosa Nova in the Thermos

bosa nova in the thermos
of the stammering though
muscular dock worker his
red and orange plaid work
shirt is a gallows
Tweetie Bird magazine
all old tobacco tins
lined up against the
lime-green firing squad
wall you'll fuel the *Yule*
with magnified drool if
you knife your stool in
front of the school

The Girl Rolling Up Her Sleeve

the girl rolling up her
sleeve in the World War II
We Can Do It! poster may
have gotten sweaty
jitterbugging to *Let's Dance*
my doesn't she have great
muscles and that
kerchief tied back on
her head resonates with
confidence and determination
she probably
drove in lots of rivets that day

Some Tropical Shadows

some tropical shadows
were having a rare book
injection ceremony in front
of the ivory and marble
resurrections of all the
five star dinner menus
wouldn't you know it
someone even thought of that
Buster Keaton gag
where the scary photo
with the black background
rocks back and forth behind
the port hole

Riverbeds' Sloshing

riverbeds' sloshing mud
slowly sheets of gray
now they are closets in
the pink trunk
used to be a goose liver
violin case for a *Mustache*
Pete from Cicero

Barn Tom

Barn Tom played his
tom-tom for *Billiard Mom*
in the *Sly Salon* until
they all got it on in
the shadow of *Two Ton*
Tessie's ton of fun

There is a Rash

there is a rash of
hasty bayonet
barn storming it
occurred during a
heavy storm on
the last day of
summer at night
it was a hammering
of rain drops it
was claptrap in
the folded nap of
the oldest cap in
the hat store
all your nonsense
is greased it's like
a brand new part
in a humming
machine the kind
of machine a mechanic
can only dream of

Lumberjack Medicine Hotel

lumberjack medicine hotel
asking for a pack of *Pall Mall*
in the *Lefty-Louie* hallway
today because loose *Luther*
More spoke furthermore on
the red priest blanket and
I'll be savoring succulent
sucking on the *Junket to*
Nowhere in my spare rice
toupee

September Jangling

September jangling jamboree
speech of three in the
sampled knee landscape
no I'm not the tortured
postal worker from *Boise*
I heard he was noisy and
dirty and a bag of carrot
slices is almost the same
as a haunted blouse drenched
in dog piss

Koala Fruit Basket

koala fruit basket hypnosis
in the final stages of tempest
arrest Oh how can you be such
a wooden darling séance in the
almond romance shadow factory
I'm *Bear Trap Hillary* happy in a
snappy pantry mansion on a
reduced pension

Predicament of the Fundamentalist

predicament of the Fundamentalist
alienist having trysts with
girls who have cysts
because malaise is fencing
with mayonnaise in a daze
so I suggest that crystal
reform takes precedence at
the dorm all cake to
the trap door, Larry!

Seemingly

seemingly
on the lake
in an ugly row boat
sure and it was a nice
crisp brown paper grocery
bag
you better get out!
wasn't it weird in
Four Sided Triangle
the way he made her?

If You Pan Cake the Panic

if you pan cake the panic
all the way into the
civilian attic clothing
see?
that's all he'll need to
get the accordion out of the
tub no warning no
warming up no! take
it to the attic!

no one will hear a thing if you turn
the faucets on full blast

Medicinal Menagerie

medicinal menagerie of the
bullring kind yes the way
that *Carmen Miranda*
would have done it with
a rebellion of head fruit
I want tobacco syrup on
my foolish toe macabre
launder mat so you better
get busy translating the
dinosaurs' diaries into *Aramaic*

A Pack of Vicious Demonic Children

a pack of vicious, demonic
children broke into *Robert*
Frost's house they beat him
to death with a wall before
burying him under snow rumor
has it that afterwards the
authorities found *Baudelaire* in
the toilet, drooling over
soiled *Can-Can* photos

Vest Voodoo

vest voodoo made me into
a battleship deck all gray
and thick metal like a
gregarious clay ice berg I
wish the equator would
make love to every ward
in all the world's mental
hospitals and turning the
vials and the dials gives
my basket some counter-clockwise
comfort

Specialty Magnet

specialty magnet
of duck chessboard warriors,
or to be naked
and the sharpest cheddar
ideals cannot stump the
eccentric meal chariots
of golden stink ideas
and *Sammy*
the Swami,
uses salami to
situate the
French
gate

Politics of the Pool Puddles

politics of the pool puddles
in the forlorn corners of
the women's lockers all of
them not only the ones
made of welded kernels of
Scottish black pepper and
someone said that there
was the decaying body of
an old motorman in the
Northwest corner of an
abandoned horror ride

Plentitude Spaceship Laughter

plenitude spaceship laughter
and it echoed loudly!
in the rafters! under the
misty mystical moon! play
the damn rubber spider
accordion, you morose *Life Magazine*!

Suppose He Came

suppose he came
out of the Shin-Dig
dream wearing nothing
but a cheaply made
wolfman mask
you would
not let a barber pole lumber
spit in the holistic
grave except for the
hallowed nectarine drivers
owned by the Japanese
solipsistic
fragrance of it, yes!
all Holland for *Mr. Hallway*
in the hollow
franchise
at sunrise,
for a surprise!

Let's Say

let's say that they
had eyebrow soup...
it was all about an
insect vaudeville routine
moving around inside the
trunk of misplaced
8mm
pirate movies
the kind they used to make
in Venezuela when
cardboard couture was the
du jour attraction not to
mention the Calypso faction
because biceps and forceps
are Chinese puzzle
cousins

Kidneys, Joe...

kidneys, Joe...
it was a parade
of sepia spittle
biscuits in a
silent film alcove
and I will
judge the clatter
accordingly

Specialized Neck Brace

specialized neck brace
veneers although I'm
not sure he can make it
all French butter, too
not noticed alloys
well well
for the boys, I mean

Safari Snuffed Out

safari snuffed out
fillings rich marmalade
into the telescope
a blurry buzz or
capped buzzard glutinous
take over! it was
a sight to
see! and with McGee?

Yonder Coined Coils

yonder coined coils of
all toil in the winding
chalk stripe suits
quite
navy blue, you know...
and seemingly nice for
fancy Nancy to darn
dainty sane solstices

Give the Moon Back

give the moon back to
semblance arrivals on the
milestone Egyptian airwaves
technical takes of *Jake*
the Clap Board
full of salty gossip
on the set of a
Valentino
picture

Tempted Tonsils in Tunisia

tempted tonsils in Tunisia
Louisa noted all so darling
monster lab pleasure of
the pressure cooking stoops

Septic Tactics

septic tactics in the
maelstrom attic of
choices *Dorsey* brothers
mumbo jumbo of *Krupa's*
tuba can life ya
all the way, Jose!

What Magnificence of Bamboo

what magnificence of
bamboo melting it was
a pelting of parrot
wigwams in the arms
of a complex roast
...and *Rococo* doctors ordered toast

You Cannot Trouble Lancelot

you cannot trouble *Lancelot*
a lake or a lot
because his denture
addiction of a ribald
East of Eden moment
such as when *Cal*
forces his brother to
"meet" his mother
becomes a *Dentyne*
benediction of gay
rumors on the set
of *Jason and the Argonauts*

Space of Wednesday

space of Wednesday so nice
and pretty lending of
lost diurnal journals in a
nocturnal urinal
such a spill of love is
like a bludgeoned box of
velvet neon I cannot
observe it Sal, and I
just don't know *Who*
Killed Teddy Bear

Belligerent Siamese Trundling

belligerent Siamese
trundling through a mermaid
forest so it is with the
utmost regret that all
specialty fructose ideas
on the mat on your mark
it's a bulwark of stapled
museums asking for zombie sex

Cannot Have Earthquake

cannot have earthquake
mission of the Burmese
cook asked Walter what
would happen if the staircase
lost its insurance policy
and I must tell you
that I have often
wondered what it would be
like if ocean bandages
transformed into curling
orange pearls or pizza
ovens in a mercurial garage

Mordant Chips of Wit

mordant
chips of wit crockery
only foolery can cause
because rash raucous
synapses duly collapsing
in the barbaric ocean
liner
stripper doldrums but for a
simulacrum
of shuddering
chowder
eaters

Clown Bark

clown bark bits all right
Easter maniac make-up
strut fortunate in the
fornicating thermometers
from Exeter we should
like to take French pastry
lessons in the Portuguese
limestone lighthouse

Neil and Me

Neil and me were peeling
pirate portraits off the
volcanic nifty *Fulbright*
Scholar nectar because
Hector fused all sane
tins of *Vagabond Sardines*
and we loved *Hecate*
the
Halloween skateboard loved
him like the waltzing
foreman in charge of all
the *Ring Ding* conveyor belts
in the *Drakes Cakes* plant

I Am An Armadillo Hostage

I am an armadillo
hostage in one of those
Mexican fortresses in
a *Leone* Western sky
Sam plan farms the *Brillo*
fuselage and win a rose
next of kin ghost dresses, sin!
leave him alone with vests
learning high

Sea of Salt

sea of salt sea of hate
dream of sea when bitter
of sea demons laughing at
sweetness of apartment
building murders in the hallway
sea of death sea of love
no master of manners of
dreaming sweet murdering sea
of me in my trunk in
my death my death my sea

Tempted Roach Box

tempted roach
box so in
Ralph sweaty
mattress laugh
they wail for
weather in
tongue of big
happy
no
face of little
night

That's It

that's it
I want something from
the *Titanic*
something
from the ocean floor

something
someone
was
using

but it lasted so long
a century of more being
a century of being able to be a
thing that exists
you still know what it is

but there's nothing
of the person who used it
except the oral tradition

of hundreds of fish

Special Code Mahogany

special code mahogany
blue of the wallowing
snifter was a shifter
and I bet nudging
won't cure a damn
thing when the disease
salesman is having a
short coffee break

Drill of the Octopus

drill of the octopus
short subject or perhaps,
as *Monsieur Verdoux* suspected,
a cranium newsreel all so
insipid yet intrepid to simply
nip the soap urine transfusion
in the bud, Zak, and
dolt *cha cha-cha*
nevermore, Lenore!

Ate Some Hateful Carbines

ate some hateful carbines
not to be mistaken for
Munchausen baking
damsels
they
swiftly caress the dress
ordeal of a plastic orangutan
that
shoulder arms!
split, like nowhere, Daddy-O!

Raspy Rasputin

raspy *Rasputin* duck bondage
magazines filled with color
pork fried rice warnings of
throat mischief and surgical
pastry conscience of a few decadent pumpkins

Mandible Japanese Matinee

mandible Japanese matinee
a giant chunk of the
turnpike frightened the parakeets
special noose flint or
fleet of foot? no! the
enema company! hehe

Jewels in the Smoke

jewels in the smoke of
the surreptitious water
pipe and I have the
knife not the one in
the water although it
would be nice to do it
on a boat
if *Muenster*
cheese flutes wax
fantastic in a plaid
Neptune basket!

Blubber of It All

blubber of it all so you
can pull planks up from
the steamy graveyard
because an old weight lifter
was shanghaied last night by
Mr. Bubbles waist of horror
all wasted late hate of
deranged medicine cabinet
lovers in a drive-in duet
of lascivious lamenting, so
don't dent my *Clark Kent*
breakfast sonata, Papa!

Spinning of Dolores

spinning of Dolores in the
junket factory mirror, I was
always a stinking octet
symposium, a Spanish column
of the possessive doldrums,
and I must say, always
symptomatic whenever severance
balcony musculature was
invoked

Stormy Looped Orange Pentameter

stormy looped orange pentameter
soup steps for poor dusty
schlep dipped in dapper
matters of peeled face
and lace for you, little
dearie, I want all fake
hostility during the rampant
Manhattan Project nightmare
voices all choices dripping malignant
valor

The Exhumation of Whimsy

the exhumation of whimsy made
certain elastic walrus's dizzy it
wasn't the nice plate of spaghetti
either, or maybe when the
roaming clappers poked their
oboes out of the sponge cake
gangplanks, some seedy furnished
room hijinks took
place in Chinatown but as
far as I know, only six thick
water bugs died on the turn table

Certain Exotic Fun

certain exotic fun awaits those
who are willing to pull apart the
urine-soaked threads of hemp rope
while a *Hammond* electric
piano plays the chords from
What I'd Say even though an
Egyptian crucifixion was hastily
being sketched and that's
why they cancelled *Jon Gnagy*
(that and because his beard
smelled like pickles from Hell)

Splendiferous Arrangement

splendiferous arrangement of
tough Turk tunics because
if even a handful of eunuchs
challenge the lozenge
workers, we will all be
punished in a bullfighter's
costume my how the
allure of greasy moonlight
can twist a young boy's
mind and tempt the corners
of his sardonically grinning
mouth!

They Forced Themselves Into My House

they forced themselves into my
house because they wanted
to put desiccated squirrel heads
in my nice ceramic cobalt
blue sugar bowl

they wanted to have sexual
relations with my nice black
and cream 1930s Bakelite radio
but I had attached a weasel femur
bone chastity lock to prevent such
vile acts from taking place

Salt On the Vague Vaseline Boats

salt on the vague Vaseline
boats and fermenting of
whatever is available at
the nadir of academic
settings because the netting
caught caution during a
portion of penitence so
I advise you to inhale
the portrait porridge
before a postal flare occurs
and we haven't got anymore Scotch

Nefarious Whistle

nefarious whistle, ah you
sad tongue all tough and
sequestered in the Northern
lights shining above the
titular tempestuous bay
of longing of songs for
laugh fins all in the
mirth of *Medoc*
because the velvet was
delivered by the sweetest
green a helmet of grasshopper
damsels roaming naked in the
shack shambles a gamble for gambols

It's the Salamander Wallpaper

it's the salamander wallpaper
that exorcises all dainty gemstone
demons with a scented red
safety derby yes we want cold
licorice stiletto pumps or maybe
Dorothy's poppies anointed with
midget droppings I cannot believe
that *Pedigree Pauline* wore a
snakeskin girdle when she mixed
the martinis for *Skinny Vinny*
I bet his hair net was vaporous

The Wonder of a Thick War Plane Factory Glove

the wonder of a thick war plane
factory glove maybe going for
a beer when the shift is over
you know there were plenty of
unwed women having heavy dates
but you just didn't hear about it too
much in the 1940s and a big
guy naked Moose took an oboe
into the junk yard they gave him
some peanuts when they
found him all the men from
the factory, I mean

Tight as a Tambourine

tight as a tambourine that's what
the screaming rancid coffee
rinds told me or it could have
been in a fleshy crow box
made out of bad glass and
incandescent whisky I'd like to
announce my silent palazzo with
arabesques of the intermezzo
the saber nature of his last
quill abreast of mint and lore

Shiny Harmony Defects

shiny harmony defects in a
sugary tungsten diatribe why
it's the sort of scandal that
any liquidity of beneficent
tornados would abjure and
so what?! I know you're
sore! you just go right back
into that "soldered" saloon and
tell *Paul Bunyon's* effeminate
fourth dimension double that
Pop-a-Matic Trouble is coming
after him in *Frosty the Snowman's*
rumba panties

Although They Were Talking

although they were talking over
a chocolate soda, it was not a
"luncheonette," I mean, strictly
speaking they all agreed to do
an infection spell on *Bell*
Pepper Hill but, suddenly, a pogo
stick had diarrhea and there
was a kind of orange slap stick
hookah in the room eating
Groucho's elephant (but not
shooting his pajamas) so it
seemed like a good time to hypnotize
the water cooler with an empty bottle
of *Veep* soda

That Has to be a Clam Pâté

that has to be a clam pâté wire
hanger yes it must have been rude to
Joan because you can see all the
cocktail sauce stains it left on
poor *Ugolino's* hips and thighs
we can jeopardize our blueprints
with Socratic napkin minnows
only if electrical face warriors
barge into the lobotomy room
and, pails in hand, start to
empty out the sea standing
forehead to mangled claw with justice
measured out by lifting up the skirt
of a gossipy saxophonist mummy

www.ingramcontent.com/pod-product-compliance
Lightning Source LLC
Chambersburg PA
CBHW022158160726
48282CB00024B/250
* 9 7 8 8 1 1 9 6 5 4 4 0 6 *